Emanuel Cole

Scriptures

of

A

Troubled

SOUL

finding the free in FREE

poetry   *Copyright 2022 © Emanuel Cole*

Not Just Alphabets Publishing

Las Vegas, Nevada

All Not Just Alphabets Publishing titles, Emanuel Cole, imprints and lines distributed are available at special quantity discounts for bulk purchases for sales promotion, fund raising, premiums, educational, institutional and library use.

Printed in the U. S. A.

Library of Congress Catalog Card Number:

ISBN:

Scriptures of A Troubled Soul

DEDICATION

I dedicate this book, first, to all the dead ends and pits I've gone through on my life's journey. Without them, there'd be no Scriptures to compose.

I dedicate this book to EVERY troubled soul I've ever encountered. Just know that you aren't forgotten.

I dedicate this book to the gutta. The gutta is where I emerged from. The gutta's voice is what my pen writes. The gutta's language is I speak fluently. And it's the gutta I bring to the poetic realm.

I dedicate this book to me. I feel, with this book, I've finally exorcised the demons from my soul that have plagued it for so many years. May these words do the same for every person that reads them.

- E. C.-

Old Testament

(My Troubled Soul)

New Testament

(Touching Troubled Souls)

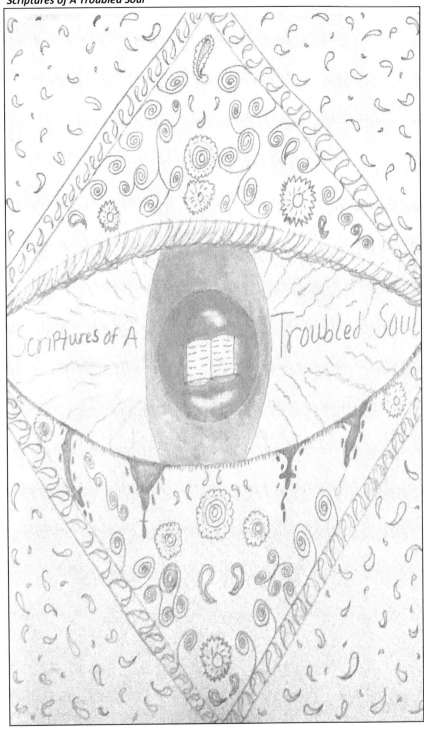

Old Testament

(My Troubled Soul)

Epiphany

If I die today

My body has given up

If I die tomorrow

Then I have procrastinated

But none of that really matters

Because I just realized

That I died yesterday

Incomplete

I lie

I steal

I cheat

I hate

I'm an uncouth degenerate

Not worthy to berate

But I love

I cry

I laugh

I feel pain

I've had a glimpse of sunshine

While standing in the rain

Please

I beg your patience

For in time

You're bound to see

A lump of clay still being molded

Into the man

I'm meant to be

Beautifully Ugly

If I write about love

I'd be denying the hate

If I said I created my destiny

I'd be denying my fate

If I write about right

You'd be blind of my wrong

But if I write about wrong

This poem would be way too long

If I paint a picture of sunshine

It wouldn't be complete without rain

And my work of art wouldn't be beautifully real

If I didn't use the colors of pain

Lost Man's Psalms

Help me God

I"m calling

Pick me up Lord

I'm falling

Has my anger

And my fears

Intertwined with

My blood and tears

Has my world caved in on me

Is everything I see

A reflection of my insanity

Why am I trapped

In this chaotic realty

If You're listening Father

Please tell me

Don't let my obsession with vengeance

Or my fostering hate

Be determining factors

For You to close the gate

I refuse to lay down

And die in shame

But I do need Your help

To beat satan at this spiritual chess game

I know You said You're coming back

I pray I'm not too late

But please

Don't make Your grand reappearance

Until You hear me say

Check mate

Lost Man's Psalms

is very special to me. It was the first real poem I ever wrote. I was seventeen, in the teen ward of a psychiatric facility. Mad at the world, and everything in it. There was a woman who came to our creative arts class who introduced writing as a real outlet. I couldn't draw, and I had no crafting skills whatsoever. I started jotting shit down all the time. When I was asked, "If you talked to God, what would the conversation sound like?" "Lost Man's Psalm" was my response. Over the years, I've revised it many times. This is the version I'm most satisfied with.

Expose

Take the earwax outta ya earholes

N listen a bit

As I expose the soul

Of the misspent energy

Of a miscreant

Hoping I ain't hellbound

Praying that I'm heaven-sent

Lookin for proof

Cause lately I ain't seein da evidence

Vengeful thoughts control my sleep

Plots n schemes invade n creep

Trying to choke out the Jesus

Who has my soul to keep

What would you do

If you knew

That even though the new you

Is the true you

The old you is willin to do what you would do

If you were true

To those who depend on you

These are the thoughts n doubts at war in my brain

But I'm only insane

If I jump back in da game

Thinkin I done mastered dis thang

The devil is just da gun

It's up to me to pull da trigga

But here I stand

A spiritual man

Instead of bein just anotha

Consciously strugglin

Nigga

Scriptures of A Troubled Soul

I picked up a pen

And put down my AK

It's how I praise

It's how I pray

It's how I celebrate

This is how I meditate

It's my sword

It's my shield

It's my chestplate

My pad testifies of my pen's saving grace

It's where I lay my life

It's where I sacrifice

It's my guiding light

It's the octagon for my spiritual fight

It's where I gained sight

It's how I was lead to day from the darkest night

But don't listen to me

Use ya ears to see

That my redemption really ain't as simple

As your religion claims it to be

Infinity War

Desperation and exasperation

Are the demons at war with the angels

Of my hopes and dreams

Tempting me with bountiful ends

In exchange for devious means

They cheer me on without words

Only maniacal glee

Rooting for the monster

Lying dormant within me

The angels plead silently

Their tears speaking thousands of words

But their hold on my heart is weakening

With each step I take toward...

Underneath It All

In my room

Alone with me

Myself and I engage in battle

Continuously and relentlessly

Vying for supremacy

Hurling accusations

Seeking a target to blame

They find me cowering

And with deadly accuracy and precision

Myself and I take aim

Throwing their ugly darts of jealousy

Insecurity

Depression and pain

As me tries to melt into a corner

Waiting for the vicious cycle

To end and begin again

Dilemma

Do real niggas go to heaven

This is the question

I present to you Reverend

If God says no

Please plead for me Reverend

There's a things

I really need you to tell Him

Like

The man that I am

Isn't always the nigga I portray

And everything I think and feel

Isn't everything I say

And even though we don't always acknowledge Him

Real niggas believe in God

Real niggs do pray

Because even though our waking hours

Are mostly spent stressing

To see another day

To real niggas is considered a blessing

If you think I'm being blasphemous

And feel no need to applaud because you're appalled

This is me

I'll always be a real nigga

When I'm never in self

Giving God applause

Cumbersome

Sometimes

The load's too heavy to bear

Sometimes

The stress is too petty to care

Sometimes

The line's too faded to see

Sometimes

Just Your presence isn't enough for me

Sometimes

The love is more painful than hate

Sometimes

It's too soon or a little too late

Naked

This is me

Struggling with my weak belief

I had to grow a whole new tree

Just to turn over a new leaf

Praying for better days

Begging for peace

But it's only during medicated sleep

That I find some relief

In my heart

So many secrets I keep

And in my mind

Nightmares loop on repeat

So I smile and I laugh

Wear the mask of a lie

For the truth is a grimace

But I refuse to cry

Lessons Yet to Learn

You gave me life

Please show me how to live

I've trained myself to take

Teach me how to give

I've cloaked myself in vengeance

Remake me to forgive

My heart has been traveling the path of hate

Lead it to the trail of love

My mind has slept on the bottom for so long

Will you wake it up to what's above

What If

If heaven was only

One mile away

Would I give up

And run that way

Or would I stand there and fight

Just one more day

Would I go there and ask God

To wipe away my tears

Or would I silently continue my journey

Swallowing my fears

I really don't know

What I'd do or what I'd say

If I were to find out that heaven

Real heaven

Was only one mile away

Rescued

Steady living in sin

Feels like I'm dying within

How could I let satan win

Before the battle begins

No longer slumbering

But still blundering

Awake in Your Spirit

I just long to be near it

I honor

Trust

Love and fear it

Now I'm begging you God

Please come and make an appearance

I've cleaned my ears

When the Gospel's whispered

I hear it

My vision is clearing

I seek Your death and ressurection

Mold me in Your perfection

Take all my faults and defections

I need Your love and correction

I need a Father

A Savior

Alpha

Omega

Creator

I hope to one day walk in Your favor

I look forward to sitting at Your table

I'll get up and shout

Saying "thank You"

Remembering

It is because of You I am able

Rescued

This poem in it's original wording was actually a verse I wrote, when I part of a Christian rap group, M.O.N. It was in the midst of creating music that this book really began to take shape. So, for their influence, many thanks and much love to Ty, Austin, Mac, Arthur Price (r.i.p.) and Col. Louis.

Inept

This seat is my haven

But it's also my hell

Created by the fires of my inactivity

Held in place by time's fading bell

I know I need to get up

But I'm lost in this state of mind

So I'll stay in this chair hoping for options more alluring

As life continues to pass me by

The Evolution of My Freedom

January 28th, 2021, marked three years since I was released from my third prison sentence, which was three years. Below, are the three biggest improvements of my life, thus far.

1. I was blessed with enough hindsight to see all the good that my mother gave to my childhood and have been privileged to be able to give that good my babies.

2. I've been able to come to grips with what manhood is, and am accepting of the weight of such a crown.

3. The core of who I call family and what family means to me, has expanded beyond my wildest dreams.

Just as things have improved, I've come to terms with the regrets I have. Thankfully, there are only three.

1. Going to prison this third time, I lost the mother of my youngest daughter, the first real female I had that And, due to that, my youngest daughter was taken by her mother's family to Mississippi. As of this writing, it's been almost seven years sine I last saw my toodybird.

2. Some of what I thought were some solid friendships faltered and fell to the weight of my prison sentence. I wish I were strong enough to hold these relationships together throughout it all.

3. It hurts my heart to not remember the names and TDCJ numbers of all the real cats I've done time with. I want to be able to represent them all individually.

The great thing, though, about evolving in freedom, is that achievements can (and will) be listed, and some regrets can (and will) be corrected and erased from the list. And I'm here to share it all.

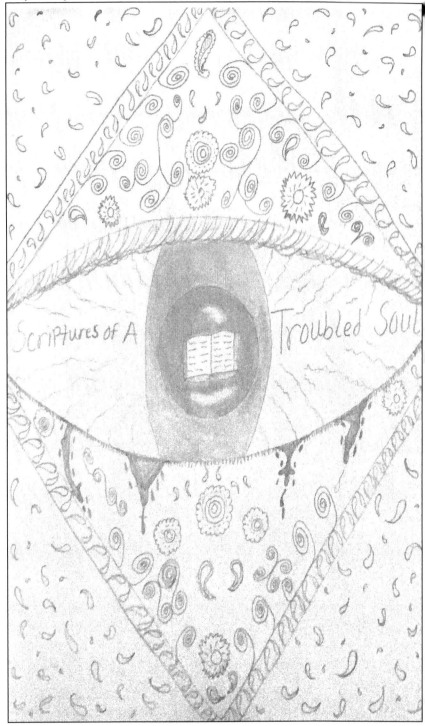

New Testament

(Touching Troubled Souls)

God's Echo

These words are mine

The universe wove em into my destiny

But they ain't just for me

These words are gifts I'm supposed to give

To everyone connected to me spiritually

The war, though, isn't between my mind

And the pad

I'm steadily fighting the angels

'Cause they keep trying to rob my ass

They want these words for themselves

To sing to their Creator

But if the words Him

And I've been with them

Then the angels must know

I'm their maker

My words are worlds where convicts are free

My words are a blunt

Light up and get high with me

My words are in battle

Keep following them in this war

And you just might die with me

If liking what you heard

Inspires you to contribute a noun or a verb

You've been imbued with power of life

But now you're forever a target

Of the angels

Who wanna take what you write

(S)He

Would your faith falter

Would you still believe

How would you feel

If He were a She

There'd be no wars

Only clashes of words

She'd be undisputedly victorious

Hers would be the last words spoken

Hers the last voice heard

Any harm brought to Her womb

Would invite Her fury and certain death

We"d vigilantly remain conscious

Of the Earth's health

Her temple would be respected

We'd take care of one another

The best we can

We inherently respect

The abodes of our mothers

While we instinctively

Test the boundaries of a man

Would we still be quick

To call a female a bitch

Sex would be the reward for selfless sacrifice

It'll be heaven on Earth

Raising the value of every human life

Making us treasure a woman's worth

Would your faith falter

Would you still believe

If you found out

He is a She

With (S)He

I was hoping to open your mind to another perspective, another possibility. I don't want to shatter anyone's core beliefs (shoutout to Col. Louis), but it is my intention to shake em up a bit.

Motives

For prized possessions

Many deeds are done

In the name of love

Many hearts are won

In the name of vengeance

Many souls are lost

In the pursuit of justice

Sometimes privacy is the cost

In the guise of sloth

Ignorance is bliss

Under the banner of the Cross

Sometimes the Bible is dismissed

In the blindness of lust

Sometime's devotion's misled

In the name of trust

Sometime's a motive is misread

I'm talking about me

But I could just as well be describing us all

How many of us living

Have not let our actions be the end all be all

Black Man

Alive from her womb

When she births I fall

I land on my feet amongst her curves

Rise and stand tall

The void of emptiness surrounds me

Flat and plain as far as my eye can see

I am the light in the midst of darkness

The calm in the midst of a raging sea

The wind's a whispering caress against my ear

With her soft-spoken command to go

With each step I take I'm surprised and awed

As my surroundings stir with life

Beginning to grow

I take a pause with a moment's epiphany

For it is then that I start to see

I am the start of all of this

The world began with me

Lessons In Life

No longer the fool

But not yet wise

Mistakes are still seen

Through experience's eyes

Pride still clouds the vision

Anger still has a voice

Making options limited

But still leaving one with a choice

Tomorrow the debt is paid in full

For actions committed today

But the height of maturity

Is finally reached

When there is a price

One's willing to pay

Chokehold

I'm addicted to this thang

It's taken over my brain

I can't explain

What it is about it that drives me insane

When I'm awake and when I sleep

When I feel good or in pain

I want it with me when I die

I'm taking it to my grave

It's got a hold and won't let go

I submit

I'm its slave

I couldn't leave it if I wanted to

Simple and plain

I admit it with this poem that I got it bad

My addiction is my pen and pad

Futile

There are things we will try to do

That just won't ever get done

There's some battles we'll fight to the death

But in spite of our strength and ferocity

Those battles will never be won

We'll love and lose

Be rejected when we choose

But living isn't futile

It's just something we've gotta do

Who We Are

There's a lot of love here

Too much to contain

There's just that much more hate

Too much for one faction to take blame

Too many fake smiles

Too many genuine tears

Too many complex agendas

Always switching gears

Endless bids for power

The mantle always exchanging hands

Be we indulge in it all

To feed our infinite demands

Faces of Death

Death comes in many colors

In a plethora of hues

Dark and light

It strikes fearlessly

When the sun shines during the day

And it stealthily preys upon us at night

It'll smile in your face

To give you closure and peace

Or guide you to hell's embrace

To ensure your torment doesn't cease

Death isn't a caricature

No one alive could play its part

For if you try to mock death's every move

It'll tear your soul apart

Sin's Defense

There's seven things they say to not do

Not unless you wanna get caught up

But after finding out

Most of what's been said are lies

I think the views of these acts

Are fucked up

Why can't I see some tits and ass

And not wanna react with my dick?

What's wrong with me being cocky

And more than confident?

Especially when I KNOW that I'm the shit

I can't be lazy?

When I've done all the work?

Why am I destined for damnation

For dishing out pain

To the author of my heart's hurt?

And I don't know about you

But I call it motivation

To see something someone has

And want the same things too

If I got ten cakes

I may wanna eat all ten right now

Just because

I don't wanna give you none

I'm now compared to a cow?

They say all these ways are sin

Being like this gone get me sent to hell

But I ain't planning

On changing my ways

So oh the fuck well

Human Nature

As the cathedral open

A strong breeze oozes in

Created by the belligerent

Stomping of the yang

Followed by the calm

Measured steps of the yin

A pre-ordained battle

In a sanctified ring

Where the winner is declared

Humanity's master and king

The first punch is thrown

Yin hits yang in eye

Yang decides to cheat

Blinds yin with a lie

Their war is eternal

Yet you and I are still slaves

To the quiet musings of the yin

And the yang's chaotic ways

Word Power

These words are mine

The universe wove em into my destiny

But they ain't just for me

These words are gifts

I'm supposed to give

To everyone connected to me spiritually

The battle, though

ain't between my mind and the pad

I'm steadily fighting the angels

Because they keep trying to rob my ass

They want these words for themselves

To sing them to their Creator

But if the words are Him

And I've been burdened with them

Then the angels must know that I'm their maker

My words are worlds where convicts are free

My words are the chronic

Roll em up n get high with me

My words are in war with what's fake

Keep following

And you just might die with me

If liking what you've heard

Inspires you to contribute

A noun or a verb

You've been gifted to control

The essence of life

But now you're forever a target

Of the angels who wanna

Take what you write

THANK YOU

This is my first book. To even say that is truly a blessing. But this blessing isn't one I alone can take credit for. There's so many peo-ple that helped to see this dream become reality. First, I wanna thank my Creator for giving me the gift of harnessing word power and for carving the path I had to trek to be able to compose my Scriptures. I want to thank my wife, Rev. Dr. Casondra Hill-Cole, for the support you've given me since Day 1. Without you, baby; none of this would even be possible. Gotta say a big THANK YOU to Moody Black and the whole 'AIN'T RIGHT TRIBE'. We AIN'T RIGHT, but we STILL HERE. Last but definitely not least, I wanna thank you, the reader for deciding to delve into my troubled soul.

-Emanuel Cole-

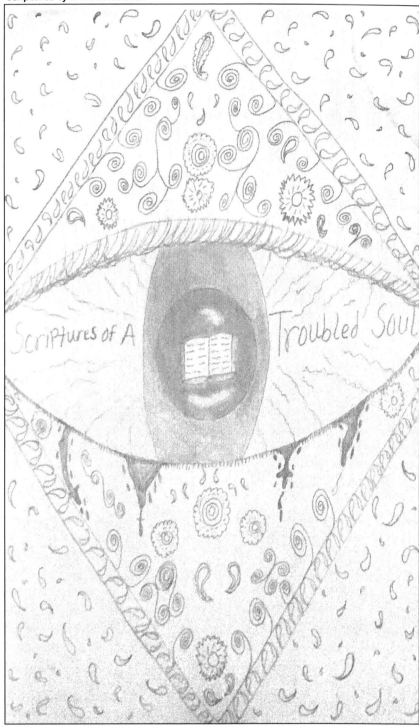

About the Author

My name is Emanuel Cole, some call me, Mr. THROWD OFF. Right now, I'm just basking in the glow of having "published" under my given name. Just gimme a second. Ok. To be honest, I never fell in love with poetry. I pimped poetry for a while. And, just in the past couple years, I began walking in love with it. The journey has been way more than worth the experiences it took to get here.

That's why I see poetry and the word power I exude through it, as my way of putting the gutta on my shoulders and bringing it to a world that's been snubbing it's nose at it for far too long. Yeah, the sewer stinks. But the sewer is everything you waste. I wanna give us the sunlight we deserve.

I'm blessed, though, to be guided by some of the greatest people to ever touch air. Shoutout to all of my Tribesmates ("Ain't Right but we Still Here!") "Who Nekkid Up In Here?!"(NAKED MINISTRIES) FAMILIATARY(movin aggressive wit a low key presence). I love each and every one of y'all.

And an extra special shoutout to every convict, gangsta, pimp, ho, c lucca, banger, jacker, hustler…

The whole gutta needs to read these poems.

Contact Information:

Founder (Throwd Off Conglomerate)

email: emanuelcole2018@gmail.com

Instagram: @ecoledapoet

Facebook: facebook.com/emanuel.cole.31

Made in the USA
Middletown, DE
16 April 2022

63925155R00035